ANTHOLOGY

First Morning

Poems About Time

For Jamie and Jeff, with love — N. S.
To Renata, Gianni e Lapo — G. M.

Barefoot Books Ltd
124 Walcot Street
Bath
BA1 5BG

First published in Great Britain in 2001 by Barefoot Books Ltd
This paperback edition published in 2003

This book was typeset in Optima and FrizQuadrata
The illustrations were prepared in china ink and watercolour
on 100% cotton 300gsm watercolour paper

Graphic design by Polka. Creation, Bath
Colour separation by Grafiscan, Verona
Printed and bound in Singapore by Tien Wah Press (Pte) Ltd

This book has been printed on 100% acid-free paper

Paperback ISBN 1-84148-338-9

British Cataloguing-in-Publication Data:
a catalogue record for this book is available from the British Library

1 3 5 7 9 8 6 4 2

First Morning

Poems About Time

compiled by Nikki Siegen-Smith

illustrated by Giovanni Manna

Barefoot Books
Celebrating Art and Story

Contents

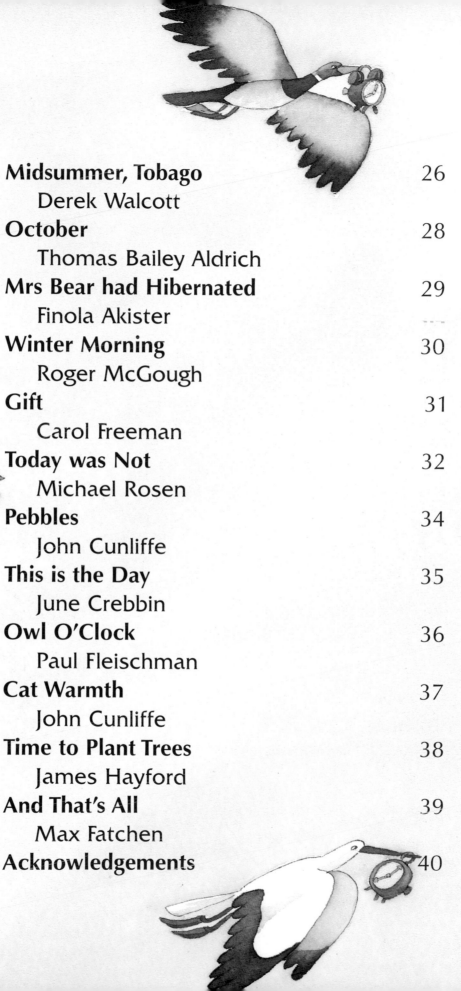

INTRODUCTION

Children like poems because they are short, because they are funny, because they rhyme and because you can write things in poems that don't really happen. One child I used to teach liked poems because, 'They make you think about things, Miss'. When I collect poems, I imagine reading them aloud to the classes of primary school children I have known, or snuggling up with my eight-year-old son at bedtime, or sharing them with other children close to me.

So this anthology on time is chosen to make you and the children in your life laugh, to set you thinking, to take you to unimagined places and to remind you of special times.

How quickly can you get your head around Jack Prelutsky's 'Today I'm Going Yesterday'? How do you feel about Philip Larkin's question? And how does your perception of time change when you read 'Earth's Clock'? If all time were a twenty-four hour clock, we have walked on earth for only thirty seconds, yet look at our impact on the world around us.

Time has a rhythm, the ticking of the clock, the movement of the sun and the changing of the seasons. Some of these poems just have fun with rhythm and sound. In 'The Bells', Edgar Allan Poe uses words to create the sounds that bells make with their 'tintinnabulation'. Does Myra Cohn Livingston's

poem make you feel that there's a cricket clock ticking beside you? It's a must to read aloud. I feel exhausted just reading Max Fatchen's 'Rushing', until I get to the last stanza where the rhythm changes to a Saturday morning laze.

Phyllis McGinley reminds us that time goes 'Hurrylikethis' or 'plod, plod, slow', just as Derek Walcott's poem 'Midsummer, Tobago' seems to capture how time can drift by without our noticing, and June Crebbin's 'Race Against Time' shows that there are 'not enough minutes in the day'.

Our lives are imprinted with remarkable times – particular seasons, festivals and holidays. Try Roger McGough's 'Winter Morning' for a slice of a snowy day, or Paul Fleischman's 'Owl O'Clock' for a helping of night. Often, most days we remember are special only for us. In 'Today was Not', we share with Michael Rosen why this day was the most special day.

I hope you will have zippy minutes, snatched hours and lazy winters reading these time poems together. And when you have had a happy day, why not follow Max Fatchen's advice in 'And That's All':

> A happy day
> Is precious to keep
> So take it to bed
> And wrap it in sleep.

Nikki Siegen-Smith

7

Today I'm Going Yesterday

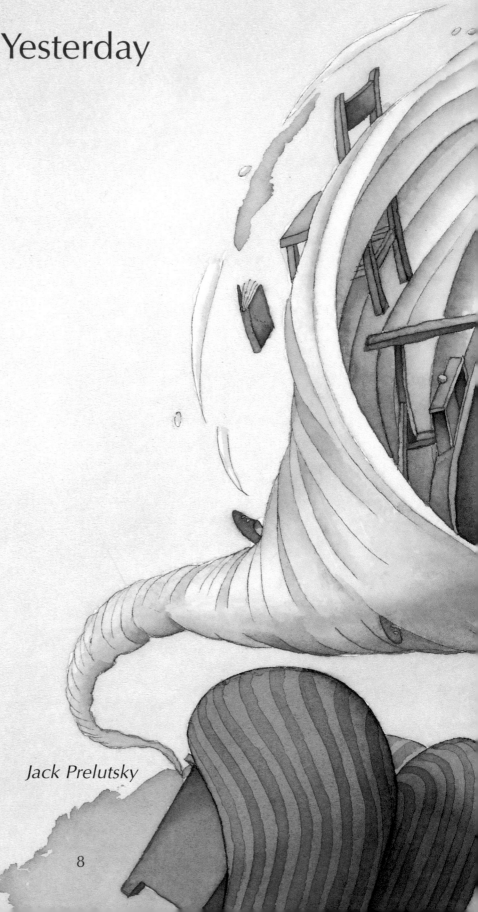

Today I'm going yesterday
as quickly as I can,
I'm confident I'll do it,
I've devised a clever plan,
it involves my running backward
at a constant rate of speed,
if I'm mindful of my timing,
I'll undoubtedly succeed.

Today I'm going yesterday,
I'm moving very fast
as I'm putting off the future
for the rather recent past,
I can feel the present fading
as I hastily depart,
and look forward to arriving
on the day before I start.

Today I'm going yesterday,
I'm slipping out of sight
and anticipate I'll vanish
just a bit before tonight,
when I reach my destination,
I'll compose a note to say
that I'll see you all tomorrow,
which of course will be today.

Jack Prelutsky

Days

What are days for?
Days are where we live.
They come, they wake us
Time and time over.
They are to be happy in:
Where can we live but days?

Ah, solving that question
Brings the priest and the doctor
In their long coats
Running over the fields.

Philip Larkin

First Morning

I was there on that first morning of creation
when heaven and earth occupied one space
and no one had heard of the human race.

I was there on that first morning of creation
when a river rushed from the belly of an egg
and a mountain rose from a golden yolk.

I was there on that first morning of creation
when the waters parted like magic cloth
and the birds shook feathers at the first joke.

John Agard

Earth's Clock

Imagine that the earth was shaped
Twenty four hours ago,
Then at 6 a.m. rains fell from the skies
To form the seas below.
At 8 a.m. in these soupy seas
The first signs of life appeared.
The dinosaurs called seventy minutes ago
But at twenty to twelve disappeared.
Man arrived just one minute ago
Then at thirty seconds to midnight,
Raised himself from his stooping stance
And started walking upright.
In the thirty seconds man's walked the earth
See what he's managed to do.

Earth's clock continues ticking;
The rest is up to you.

Pat Moon

12

13

There isn't Time!

There isn't time, there isn't time
To do the things I want to do,
With all the mountain-tops to climb,
And all the woods to wander through,
And all the seas to sail upon,
And everywhere there is to go,
And all the people, every one,
Who lives upon the earth, to know.
There's only time, there's only time
To know a few, and do a few,
And then sit down and make a rhyme
About the rest I want to do.

Eleanor Farjeon

from Circle One

Nothing happens only once,
Nothing happens only here,
Every love that lies asleep
Wakes today another year.

Owen Dodson

from The Bells

Keeping time, time, time,
In a sort of Runic rhyme,
To the tintinnabulation that so musically wells
From the bells, bells, bells, bells, bells.

Edgar Allan Poe

Crickets

they	tell
the	time
of	night
they	tick
the	time
of	night
they	tick
they	tell
of	night
they	tick
and	tell
the	time
they	tick
they	tell
the	time
they	click

Myra Cohn Livingston

Off to Outer Space Tomorrow Morning

You can start the Count Down, you can take a last look;
You can pass me my helmet from its plastic hook;
You can cross out my name in the telephone book —
　　For I'm off to Outer Space tomorrow morning.

There won't be any calendar, there won't be any clock;
Daylight will be on the switch and winter under lock.
I'll doze when I'm sleepy and wake without a knock —
　　For I'm off to Outer Space tomorrow morning.

I'll be writing no letters; I'll be posting no mail.
For with nobody to visit me and not a friend in hail,
In solit'ry confinement as complete as any gaol
　　I'll be off to Outer Space tomorrow morning.

When my capsule door is sealed and my space-flight has begun,
With the teacups circling round me like the planets round the sun,
I'll be centre of my gravity, a universe of one,
    Setting off to Outer Space tomorrow morning.

You can watch on television and follow from afar,
Tracking through your telescope my upward shooting star,
But you needn't think I'll give a damn for you or what you are
    When I'm off to Outer Space tomorrow morning.

And when the rockets thrust me on my trans-galactic hop,
With twenty hundred light-years before the first stop,
Then you and every soul on earth can go and blow your top —
    For I'm off to Outer Space tomorrow morning.

Norman Nicholson

Rushing

Rush, rush,
Race, race.
Teeth to brush,
Wash your face.

Eat your toast,
Drink your cup,
For goodness' sake,
Hurry up.

Where's my bag?
On the chair.
Quick, quick,
Comb your hair.

Shoes done,
Fuss, fuss.
Run, run,
School bus.

Books turn.
Weary brain,
Learn, learn.
Home again.

It's wonderful
To laze away,
Sleeping in
On Saturday.

Max Fatchen

Race Against Time

And here we are now,
Ready for the start,
Pencils poised,
Breathing heavily,
Eyes on the starter...
And they're off!

Four fives, two fives, three fives,
Eight fives —
Eight fives? Eight fives?
FORTY!
And they're
Over that one
And on to the next —
And coming up now
To the half-minute mark.
Half a minute,
Half a minute to go
And one of them is trailing —
No, no,
He's still there
He's still in the race —
Nine fives, nine fives?
Nine fives?
FORTY-FIVE!
And into the straight,
Down the paper,
And they're
Coming up to the finish
With five seconds to go,
Four, three, two —
And they've finished!
With a second to spare
And they're
Breathing freely now,
Papers over,
Pencils down.

June Crebbin

Lengths of Time

Time is peculiar
And hardly exact.
Though minutes are minutes,
You'll find for a fact
(As the older you get
And the bigger you grow)
That time can
Hurrylikethis
Or plod, plod, slow.

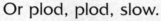

Waiting for your dinner when you're hungry?
Down with the sniffles in your bed?
Notice how an hour crawls along and crawls along
Like a snail with his house upon his head.

But when you are starting
A game in the park,
It's morning,
It's noon,
And suddenly it's dark.
And hours like seconds
Rush blurringly by,
Whoosh!
Like a plane in the sky.

Phyllis McGinley

Midsummer, Tobago

Broad sun-stoned beaches.

White heat.
A green river.

A bridge,
scorched yellow palms

from the summer-sleeping house
drowsing through August.

Days I have held,
days I have lost,

days that outgrow, like daughters,
my harbouring arms.

Derek Walcott

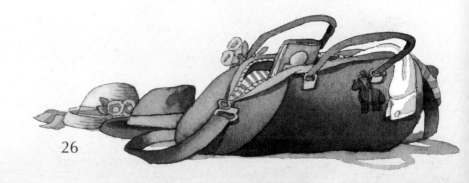

October

October turned my maple's leaves to gold;
      The most are gone now; here and there one lingers.
Soon these will slip from out the twig's weak hold,
      Like coins between a dying miser's fingers.

Thomas Bailey Aldrich

Mrs Bear had Hibernated

Mrs Bear had hibernated
All the winter through.
She went to bed and slept a lot,
There was nothing else to do.
The ground was cold and frozen hard,
The winds were fierce and chill,
So she and little Baby Bear
Slept on and on, until
One morning Mrs Bear woke up
And she said to herself, said she,
'I think the sun is shining,
I'll just pop out and see.'
So Baby Bear and Mrs Bear
Got up and left their den,
Outside the snow was falling fast
So they went back in again.
'I fear, my dear,' said Mrs Bear,
'It's really very plain,
We have woken up too early.'
So they went to sleep again.

Finola Akister

Winter Morning

Winter
morning.
Snowflakes
for breakfast.
The street
outside
quiet
as a
long
white
bandage.

Roger McGough

Gift

Christmas morning i
got up before the others and
ran
naked across the plank
floor into the front
room to see grandmama
sewing a new
button on my last year
ragdoll.

Carol Freeman

Today was Not

Today was not
very warm
not very cold
not very dry
not very wet.

No one round here
went to the moon
or launched a ship
or danced in the street.

No one won a great race
or a big fight.

The crowds weren't out
the bands didn't play.

There were no flags no songs
no cakes no drums.
I didn't see any processions.
No one gave a speech.

Everyone thought today was ordinary,
busy busy
in out in
hum drummer day
dinner hurry
grind away day.

Nobody knows that today
was the most special day
that has ever ever been.

Ranzo, Reuben Ranzo,
who a week and a year ago was gone
lost
straying starving
under a bus? in the canal?
(the fireman didn't know)
was here, back,
sitting on the step
with his old tongue lolling,
his old eyes blinking.

I tell you —
I was so happy
So happy I tell you
I could have grown a tail —
and wagged it.

                    Michael Rosen

Pebbles

We collect days,
Like a boy collecting pebbles
On the beach.

Suddenly his pockets are heavy.

Suddenly, we are old.

John Cunliffe

This is the Day

This is the sort of day
I should like to wrap
In shiny silver paper
And only open when it's raining,

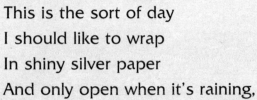

This is the sort of day
I should like to hide
In a secret drawer to which
Only I have the key,

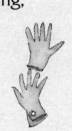

This is the sort of day
I should like to hang
At the back of the wardrobe
To keep me warm when winter comes,

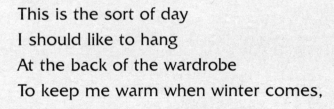

This is the day
I should like to last for ever,

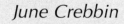

This is my birthday.

June Crebbin

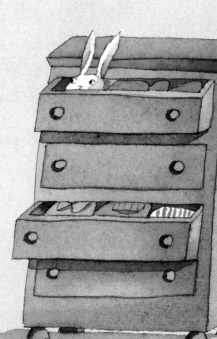

Owl O'Clock

On summer nights I sleep in the treehouse,
far from our grandfather clock's deep chime.
My watch is back in my room. I don't mind.
I see and hear and smell the time.

Frog o'clock,
then first star,
porch lights on,
then jasmine scent.
Cats called in,
then porch lights out,
the evening's final bus
up Ninth,
and then my favourite time of all,
the hour after racoon-prowl,
the time I love to listen for —
owl o'clock at night.

Paul Fleischman

Cat Warmth

All afternoon,
My cat sleeps,
On the end of my bed.

When I creep my toes
Down between the cold sheets,
I find a patch of cat-warmth
That he's left behind;
An invisible gift.

John Cunliffe

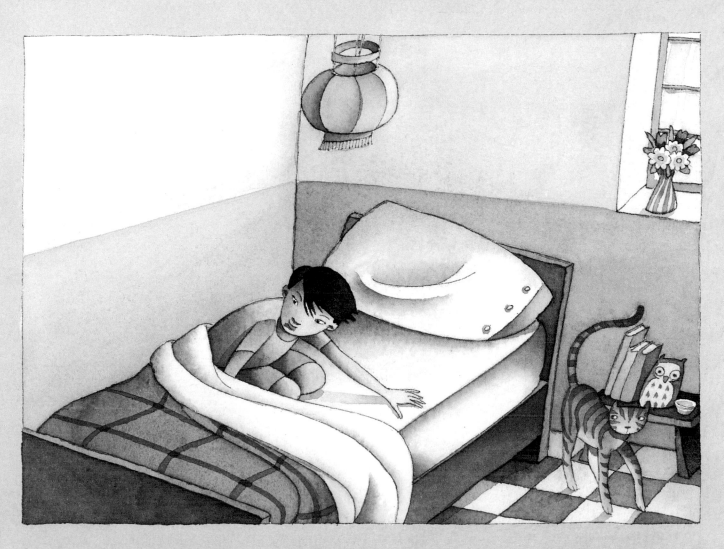

Time to Plant Trees

Time to plant trees is when you're young
So you will have them to walk among —

So aging, you can walk in shade
That you and time together made.

James Hayford

And That's All

A happy day
Is precious to keep
So take it to bed
And wrap it in sleep.

Max Fatchen

ACKNOWLEDGEMENTS

'Today I'm Going Yesterday' from *Something BIG Has Been Here*, copyright © Jack Prelutsky 1990. Published in the UK by Heinemann Young Books, an imprint of Egmont Children's Books Limited, London and used with permission; 'Days' from *The Whitsun Weddings*, copyright © Philip Larkin 1964, reproduced by kind permission of Faber & Faber Ltd; 'First Morning' from *Laughter Is An Egg*, copyright © John Agard 1990. Published by Viking; 'There isn't Time!' from *Something I Remember* by Eleanor Farjeon, copyright © Gervase Farjeon. Published by Puffin Books; 'Circle One' from *Powerful Long Ladder*, copyright © Owen Dodson. Reprinted by permission of Farrar, Straus and Giroux, LLC; 'Crickets' reprinted with the permission of Margaret K. McElderry Books, an imprint of Simon & Shuster Children's Publishing Division, from *I Never Told and Other Poems* by Myra Cohn Livingston. Copyright © Myra Cohn Livingston 1992. By permission also of Marian Reiner; 'Off to Outer Space Tomorrow Morning' from *Collected Poems*, copyright © Norman Nicholson 1984. Published by Faber & Faber Ltd. Copyright © Norman Nicholson; 'Rushing' from *Peculiar Rhymes and Lunatic Lines* by Max Fatchen. First published in the UK by Orchard Books in 1995, a division of The Watts Publishing Group Limited, 96 Leonard Street, London EC2A 4XD. Copyright © Max Fatchen 1995; 'Race Against Time' from *The Jungle Sale*, copyright © June Crebbin 1988. First published by Viking Kestrel 1988; 'Lengths of Time' copyright © 1965, 1966 by Phyllis McGinley. Copyright renewed 1993, 1994 by Patricia Blake. First appeared in *Wonderful Time*, published by J.B. Lippincott (now HarperCollins Publishers). Reprinted by permission of Curtis Brown, Ltd.; 'Midsummer, Tobago' from *Collected Poems: 1948-1984* by Derek Walcott. Copyright © 1986 by Derek Walcott. Published by Faber & Faber Ltd.; 'Mrs Bear had Hibernated' (p 53, 20 lines) from *Before you go to Bed* by Finola Akister illustrated by Colin West, (Viking Kestrel,1989) Reproduced by kind permission of Penguin Books Ltd. Copyright © Finola Akister 1989; 'Winter Morning' (no. iii of 'Snow and Ice Poems') from *Sky in the Pie* by Roger McGough, (Kestrel 1983). Copyright © Roger McGough 1983; 'Gift' by Carol Freeman from *Black Fire* ed. Leroi Jones and Larry Neal, copyright © Carol Freeman. Reprinted by permission of Sterling Lord Literistic; 'Today was Not' by Michael Rosen from *Wouldn't You Like To Know?* Published by Puffin Books 1981. Copyright © Michael Rosen 1977, 1981; 'Pebbles' (5 lines) from *Standing on a Strawberry* by John Cunliffe, (André Deutsch Ltd 1987). Copyright © John Cunliffe 1987; 'This is the Day' from *The Dinosaur's Dinner* by June Crebbin (Viking, 1992). Copyright © June Crebbin 1992; 'Owl O'Clock' copyright © Paul Fleischman; 'Cat Warmth' (8 lines) from *Standing on a Strawberry* by John Cunliffe, (André Deutsch 1987). Copyright © John Cunliffe 1987; 'Time to Plant Trees' from *Star in the Shed Window: Collected Poems 1933-1988* by James Hayford; 'And That's All' from *Peculiar Rhymes and Lunatic Lines* by Max Fatchen. First published in the UK by Orchard Books in 1995, a division of The Watts Publishing Group Limited, 96 Leonard Street, London EC2A 4XD.

The publishers have made every effort to contact holders of copyright material. If you have not received our correspondence, please contact us for inclusion in future editions.